Bread and Milk and Music:
Three Sisters' Voices

Foreword by John C. Rezmerski

Karen K. Gibson
Helen K. Beaman
Mary K. Boyack

POEMS BY

Karen Keith Gibson

Helen Keith Beaman

Mary Keith Boyack

Bread and Milk and Music, first edition
September 2007
Printed in the United States
by Press Media, Provo, Utah

Book and cover design
by Stacy Schwantes Keith.

The front cover is from a painting by T. Todd Knell.

The publication of this book was made possible
by a grant from
Frank L. and Belinda Boyack VanderSloot.

ISBN 978-0-9713882-7-7   U.S. $12.00

Contents

This book is dedicated to
our mentor, friend, brother—

Max C. Golightly
May 19, 1924 to April 10, 1997

—who awakened the poet in each of us.

Acknowledgements

We wish to thank:

Richard H. Cracroft for his careful reading of our manuscript and for his kind words and encouragement,

John Rezmerski for demanding, "Where's your book?" which impelled us into this publishing project, for egging us on, and for writing the Foreword.

Sue Chambers for inviting us to travel to Minnesota to read our poetry, which gave us courage to move forward.

Rosalyn Ostler for proofreading with her gimlet eye and for our enduring friendship.

The members of ScanCelts and the Pine Nuts for giving suggestions and workshops that fine-tune our poetry, and for sharing their own stunning works.

The Word Weavers, members of our local chapter of the Utah State Poetry Society for their support and friendly encouragement.

The many friends we have made in the National Federation of State Poetry Societies.

Stacy Schwantes Keith, our niece, who designed the book.

Allan J. Keith, our nephew who acted as our manager and advisor through the printing phase of this undertaking.

Our Families: husbands, brothers, sisters, children and all who have given us support and stories that form the basis for some of our poems.

The authors wish to recognize and thank the editors of the following journals in which some of these poems have been previously published.

Utah Sings:
"Rest in West Virginia," "Eight Loaves," "Tell Mama to Wait"

Encore:
"Eight Loaves," "Rest in West Virginia," "Grandma, My Midwife" earlier title: "Midwife," "I Haven't Called You Lately"

ByLine: "Pendulum"

Beverly Keith Golightly

Last of all and first of all, appreciation for our sister Beverly who breathes life into the words original, unique, and even eccentric. Her poetry weaves words into collages of sound and meaning, pierces the edges of memory and wonder. She has taught us the art spirit that embodies every aspect of her life. And thanks for bringing Max into our lives.

Forward: The Art of Gratitude

That poetic genius John Berryman once wrote:

> . . . my mother told me as a boy (repeatingly)
> 'Ever to confess you're bored
> means you have no
> Inner Resources.' I conclude now I have no
> inner resources, because I am heavy bored.

Mary, Helen, and Karen Keith's mother might have had the same idea, but had the resolve of a woman who not only said, but did, and who could rely on the stability of a family unafflicted by the dysfunctions of Berryman's. Karen writes:

> The words I'm bored echoed
> through my Mother's house.
> Once!

Her mother's solution to boredom was work, a project shared by the whole family, followed by an active appreciation of nature. None of that nonsense about inner resources. It was taken for granted that resources observed and shared would be transformed into inner strength. "And," to quote another famous poet, "that has made all the difference."

You can't read many pages from the hands of Karen, Helen, and Mary without understanding how they forged their sisterhood in a household full of resourceful siblings, with parents who functioned as parents, and who all together shared a sense of the generations from which they proceeded, and love for the community in which they continue to grow, to appreciate each other's work, and to pass their awareness on to their own children and grandchildren, and to their friends.

That's what this book is about. It's full of poems about growing up during lean times, about learning and struggling to prosper, about a past crowded with duties and pastimes that have now escaped us (or sometimes, from which we are gratefully escaping). Some of the trappings of those times evoke nostalgia—galvanized washtubs, starched lace curtains stretched on wood drying-frames, bread baked in a coal stove, flour-sack dish towels, keeping a cow. But this is not a "good old days" book. Some of the poems bring back old sadness—leg braces on kids with polio, drought, heavy labor for children, having to grudgingly accept, on rare occasions, government commodity handouts. The heart of the book is the family's resilience, their creativity, and insistent caring. They present all this without self-righteousness or preaching or platitudes. Their book documents the life and times of the Keith family, recording not just physical details and events, but more vitally the feelings that overflow from them. The aim is understanding and empathy.

That's the heart of the book, the experience it comes from. What about its art?

What turned these three sisters not just into spirited women but into such fine poets, three such distinctive voices that harmonize like a trio? How did this book come to be? As you'll discover in reading the poems, the Keith family was blessed with talent, and always liked being around talented people. The three sisters' parents were involved in presenting plays around the towns in their home area. Their mother, Lavon, was a talented and creative seamstress and a woman who could use whatever was available to improvise toys, decorations, and useful items. Helen describes her as "a natural teacher." Their father, Bill, by turns and by necessity a woodcutter, a carpenter, a farmer, and a steel mill worker, had a gift for coaxing fruit out of arid soil. Their older sister, Beverly, is an artist as well as a poet. It was Beverly's husband, the widely admired poet and mentor Max Golightly, who in the early 90s introduced first Mary, then Karen, to the world of serious poetry, showing them how to hone their craft. Then Helen, who had dabbled in poetry for most of her life, got serious and joined them. It was a world in which they could thrive. As Karen's biographical note in volume eight of Utah Sings puts it, "She was the seventh of eight children caught in a whirlwind of talent, searching for a place. When she discovered poetry, she was home at last." Indeed she was, and is.

By the late 90s, all three of them were active members of the Utah State Poetry Society and were entering the rigorous contests sponsored by the state organizations that make up the National Federation of State Poetry Societies. They attended workshops. They sought criticism from experts and amateurs alike, always seeking ways to intelligently engage their readers. Boredom was unthinkable. They refused to settle for the confessional or sentimental or joking modes of poetry, and explored the documentary and celebratory modes. They practiced, together and separately. They worked.

In 2003, in Sioux Falls, S.D., at the NFSPS national convention, a poem of Karen's took a prize in one of the contests, a poem written from the point of view of a pioneer woman. It is customary for the awardees to read their winning poems to the assemblage. It was, in my opinion, the most emotionally powerful poem I had heard that day. After the session was over, I made sure to tell her so, and we spent an hour or so in conversation about poetry and life. That's when I found out that Karen and Helen were sisters (earlier in the day, I had been introduced to Helen after a presentation I had given). That evening, they invited me to join the group at their table, and introduced me to several other Utah poets, which led to my being included in a late night read-around that continued the next night, and continued the following year in Columbus, Ohio, and at more meetings over the next few years. I stayed included.

Which is how I came to be riding in Mary's car last March along with Karen and Helen, and our friend Rose Ostler, headed from Provo to St. George to participate in the RedRock Writer's Workshop.

The Keith sisters presented a program of family poems that led me to ask, "Where's your book?" That elicited bright smiles from them and from my fellow Minnesotan Susan Chambers who seconded the motion. They had been considering the idea for a couple of years. A little compliment, a little teasing query, a look of expectation, friendship with talented poets—it all nudges the world another step forward into beauty. It feels good. Eventually I was invited to write this foreword.

I do not tell this to seek any credit in the matter. Destiny is destiny and needs no help from wandering Minnesotans. My motive in telling it is to set up a platform from which to explain a bit more about the art which has been at work for decades in making this book so brilliantly possible.

When Mary drives, Mary drives. There's a bag of healthful snacks on the console, a supply of CDs, and a sense of being on a quest. Our friend Rita Bowles says, "Mary can guide you into assorted states of consciousness and it's huge fun if you have an active imagination." Helen, she says, is "a short package of dynamite," while Karen is "the yeast in our communal loaf, and we all rise to her occasions with laughter." But it's also true that Mary is very much in the moment, Helen is gentle, and Karen is a very contemplative person.

So there I was, a passenger in paradise, headed for a poetry conference, riding through some of the most beautiful country on the planet. We talked about poetry. And there was some singing—a bit of continuation of the sing-along held at Mary's place the night before. And then Karen saying, "Let's play Mary's gratitude game."

The gratitude game is simple. The participants take turns saying things they are grateful for. Perhaps in a single word: "babies." Or in a more elaborate fashion: "the way the snow goes off the hills and leaves those white lines that look almost like writing." Or in an immediate appetitive way: "these strawberries." Perhaps in a meditative vein: "the sacrifices our ancestors made to make it possible for roads to take us almost anywhere we need to go." Responses may be totally serious ("good schools"), playful ("saddle horses"), or completely frivolous ("anything blue"). Some are unclassifiable: "Gabby Hayes."

The point is simply to express gratitude, often for things that have not been singled out for praise before. Any remark is likely to generate a little conversation extending or elaborating the reasons for such appreciation. It's not enough to feel grateful, it's necessary to articulate your gratitude.

That's the origin of the art you experience in the celebratory poems of this book. Three voices that have practiced harmony till it's second nature do their own riffs on family motifs. They take turns for solos, savor the memories of the people they love and the games they've played together, the perceptions they agree on, the different interpretations of the same material.

We readers are absorbed by the game, and we get to say, "I'm grateful for having this world opened up to my attention." I'm grateful for Mary's hospitality, Helen's scrutiny, Karen's playful and welcoming spirit. And for the family that nurtured their talents. And for so many meticulously crafted poems. And for the music that undergirds it all. And above all, for their careful commitment to finding the right words, and delight in their discoveries. I'm grateful that you get to experience this book.

You can't just come along for the ride—the homeward journey is too full of opportunities to practice the art of gratitude.

John Calvin Rezmerski
Mankato, Minnesota
August 28, 2007

Family members referred to in the poems.

Barbara Tope, Barbry
> Our great, great grandmother

William J. Keith, Jr., Willie, Bill, Dad
> Our father

William J. Keith, Sr., Big Will
> Willie's father, our grandfather.

Isabella, Mamma
> Willie's mother, our grandmother

Lavon, Mama
> Our mother

Grandma Knighton
> Our mother's grandmother

Grandma Penrod
> our mother's mother

Children of William and Lavon
> J. Alan Keith
> Beverly Keith Golightly
> William P. Keith, Bill, Billy
> Mary Belle Keith Boyack
> Wayne P. Keith
> Helen Keith Beaman
> Karen Keith Gibson
> Lon P. Keith, Lonnie

Max C. Golightly
> Beverly's husband

Preface:
My Sisters' Stories

My sisters' stories are also mine, yet Karen's voice speaks uniquely eloquent echoes of our childhood. Mary's voice vibrates with her own timbre, generation of melody to counterpoint memory. My stories are metal mined from my own quarry refined by my experience. Our tales, as liquid as milk, as substantial as bread, grow up from the rich soil of our parents' lives to nourish us. We sing our emptiness, our fullness with a generous twist of lyrical license. What is not true is still truth.

We have cut across the same vacant lot on the way to the same schools, had some of the same teachers, tended the same children, and, in more than one case, had the same boy friend. No one has written that poem yet.

So, dear Reader, dear Listener, please sit down with us around our kitchen table, and accept this offering of Bread and Milk and Music, taken with a few grains of salt.

Helen Keith Beaman, Editor

Bread and Milk and Music:
Three Sisters' Voices

Walking the Salty Sea

This religion, young like the boy-prophet,
declares a new order. God gives
no reason in this season of budding,
no whys.

In 1849 Oliver is called; Eliza consents.
She rides in the wagon with her husband
and his soon-to-be second wife,
to this place, this valley,
where Brigham will officiate.
She wears her mended calico
worn and dreary as the endless days
of July's untamed dust.

Carrie, dressed in white, her youth blooming
with each roll of the wheels,
sits in the middle of the marriage.
How long before she wilts like flowers
on faded dresses, like flowers left too long
on mounds sheltering loved ones,
calendared too long on some forsaken plain?

Cloaking sage and remnants of withered wheat,
gloaming welcomes home the bonded threesome.
Eliza bakes the cornbread, slices smoked ham,
scrambles just-gathered eggs. While they eat
she busies herself with discontented children,
with chores content to wait.

Suffocating silence boomerangs the log walls,
rises to loft and back again. Dying candles
create shadows, romance the room,
shiver the anticipation.

I'll milk now . . . Eliza treads dusk's fading trail
to the cow shed. With her soiled apron she
wipes flushed cheeks, smothers escaping sobs.

There, blanketed in black, she hangs
hungry arms around the neck, nestles her head
against the Guernsey coat

and moans until the pain subsides.
– Karen

Rest in West Virginia

On her way
from Pennsylvania to Kentucky,
Great, Great Grandma Barbry Tope
stopped at Harper's Ferry.
Her family stopped
because Barbry was sick with the fever.
Some folks by name of McDonough
put her on a cot by their fireplace,
made room for the others
in one end of the barn.
Her Ma sat there for most of two weeks
bathin' her girl's arms and forehead,
tryin' to get raspberry tea down her,
while Pa set about mendin'
everything he could find:
harnesses, shoes for the horses
and for the folks. Sharpenin' knives.
It was too early in March
for gettin' the ground ready for plantin'.
Skies were the color of the gray wool blanket
that scratched her chin as she tossed
side to side like she was still ridin' on the ferry.
Snow came and went like a bashful suitor

who couldn't make up his mind.
Then one mornin', spring
shone in the window. Four days later,
they figured Barbry was strong enough to go.
As the wagon started meanderin'
like a ribbon snake on the road
up toward the Appalachians,
Barbry looked back to see the blossoms
just beginnin' to burst on the dogwood trees
and young Robert McDonough
wavin' his hat.

— *Helen*

Note: The two preceding poems are fictionalized.

Willie Brings His Daddy Home

Willie, barely five, shivers against the window,
can feel drops splatter through the glass
that shields him from the storm.
Through rain and waviness of the panes,
he sees a father robin shake away the wet,
fluff wing feathers to cover nested chicks.
Mother bird hovers above,
dives like lightning, down then back.
A worm dangles as she dances
side to side on the branch.

A scarf of clouds muffles day,
stretches fingerlike fringes
to drench the earth. Mamma lights
the coal oil lamp.
She waits, her back to the fire,
strains toward the door whenever
wagon wheels crunch the damp gravel.

Willie. . .?
Okay!

His voice scratches like chalk on his slate.
He hurries to get his coat that Mamma
cut down from Grandma's
after she died, turned it inside out.
Now the storms of all those years
rub against his skin. Once outside
he leans into the rain, lets it sting his face,
slows at Silver's Beer Hall.
Droplets sneak down his back.

Those men aren't the same as at church,
their faces and eyes red, voices loud.
They laugh as Big Will spins stories.
Mamma told Aunt Mattie,
That's when his Irish shows.
Willie strides in, Big Will jokes about him,
tells a few more stories,
gulps the brown, sour-smelling brew,
hurls back words, —*li'l man,*
one day,—*Ya'all jist watch,*—
laughs his way out the door.

Willie says he'll ride
in the back of the wagon
to keep the logs from shifting.
He won't let his Dad see him cry.
The sharp ache of the razor strop
never hurt this much.
Rain still slides down the sky.
– Helen

4

Missing Lines

I search for the grandmother
who died too soon to hang a memory on.
The family photograph fails to capture more
than one stark and stilted flash,
a final sitting before she was too weak
to sit, before she was—

Daddy, not yet six, stands
behind the others. I see pain
in his face. Bess hid his shoes,
but it's more than that.
The three sisters cluster like the Pleiades
around Grandmother's knee.
The pain in her face is *because*—

I search, trying to pry loose
her mask of mortality. That shell,
closing too soon on her life,
also hides *us* from ourselves.
Grandchildren will scan my image,
wondering what I never knew myself.
– Helen

Willie

nine years-old, rubs his toe
across the knot worn smooth
on the plank floor in front of the counter.
He waits for Grandma's flour.

Hey, Utah,
how many wives huz your daddy got?

Mr. Cutchins' tobacco smoke billows,
hangs where he wheezes it into the air

as he counts coins. He bellows
like a barker at the carnival,
teases folks from the corners
to see the Mormon boy.
Customers' laughter echoes his,
bounces around shelves
of calico and denim, tobacco, salt,
liniment and peppermint,
barrels of pickles, crackers, dried corn,
the stove with its empty belly.
Echoes that pummel
Willie's shrinking space.

Ashville dust puffs between his toes
as he hurries home to Grandma's house.
Humid air weighs him down
like the sack of flour growing heavier,
pressing on his heart.
Carolina heat simmers the tears
on his cheeks,
penetrating,

but not to February's grief
frozen in him like the Utah earth
they hacked and hoed
to dig his Mamma's grave.
– Helen

Homestead at Buckhorn

Not a tree in sight, just sagebrush,
rabbit brush, June grass—
where they homesteaded in 1915,
his pa and new stepmother.
Dad was eleven years old
with four younger sisters.

Beyond are hills where Big Will
took him to cut firewood
to sell as far away as Parowan.
Willie studied his father,
matched his movements.
He swung back, gathering energy,
then at the top of the arc
threw his weight into it,
angling the axe so it struck exact strokes.

He helped "prove up" the farm
with his four-horse team
and double-disk John Deere plow.
He spoke fondly of his horses
Dolly, Old Pete, and Dan,
but wouldn't give two cents
for that stubborn old mule.

He wasn't heavy enough
to weigh down the grader
he stood on behind the plow.
He'd pile big boulders beside him
to help smooth the dry, hard ground.
They sometimes shifted
bruising his legs and ankles.

He worked like a man tackling roots
and stones, went back over the ground
until the dirt lay calm as carded wool,
then sculpted brown rippling furrows.

He longed for shade of a cottonwood,
or even the tall skinny shadow
of a Lombardy poplar—
thirst for trees surpassed
only by thirst for his father's praise.
- Helen

Mama's Kiss

In the professional photograph,
she is fifteen, maybe seventeen,
before marriage on her
eighteenth birthday. The fringe of hair
a tease above her eyebrows, blue eyes bright
even through sepia. Hair, a bouffant puff,
swings toward her neck just above
her jaw line. I think her hair is bobbed.
Daddy, eyes and voice softening to violet, says,
Why no, her hair came clear down
to her waist.

Now I see that walk,
their feet dusting the empty road.
She stops just this side
of a pear tree. Blossoms like
white moths, tempted by the night's light,
flutter down to perfume her hair.
Branches draw a mosaic across the moon,
its rays bright upon her cheek
as she turns, just so, lifting her chin
to the sky and to him for that first kiss.
– Helen

Love Nest

A shell of an outbuilding inclines toward ruin.
That was your parents' first house,
Uncle Lloyd tells me,
built in the first place for Uncle Joe Bidwell,
moved here from its spot
at the foot of the sandhill.
We been usin' it for storage.

I look.

8

It can't measure more than eight feet by ten.
smaller than the hay wagon parked next to it.
Where did they put the bed?

I remember hearing Dad tell of building
a lean-to addition on the cabin frame
for a kitchen. How proud he was
when he bought a cook stove
from Jim White and hauled it home.
To make, he mused,
a snug, comfortable love nest.
– Mary

Grandma, My Midwife

For Mama   May, 1925

The moon, a silver apple,
rises full and fat
before the sun goes down.
Grandma Knighton sees it
without even looking up.
You'll have your baby tonight.
Her midwife eyes pat my roundness,
my full moon protruding
under the folds of fabric.
Well, I won't.

Grandma walks down the sand hill
in the high, bright gold of moon,
arrives before the doctor.
We didn't send for her.
She knows when to come, what to ready.
She cleans a second time
as water boils, herb tea brews;
smoothes blankets in the crib,
rubs my feet, then supports my back

as the pains intensify.
Doctor Curtis comes in time for the delivery.
When he sees the baby's blue face,
the cord braiding his neck,
he sighs, sets him aside and cares for me.
Grandma shakes her head,
moves quickly to the ten-pound baby,
limp as yesterday's picked lilacs.
Too big for your first,
and you not weighing a hundred pounds.

Grandma breathes into his mouth,
cleans and massages,
as a cat licking life into her kittens;
pays no attention when the doctor leaves,
commands life into the lungs.
Inky fingers turn pink,
legs and feet kick into color.
His face reddens as he crows and squawks
his greeting to life, then coos,
as she places him to my breast.

She turns down the lamp,
settles into the rocking chair.
Thanks dampen my cheeks.
She'll stay until it's time to leave.
Only she knows when that will be.
– Helen

Mary Be-elle

It's probably time
for my dose of cod liver oil.
I'd rather keep hop-scotching.
My lack of response to her call
brings Mama to the yard, hands on hips.

I decide I'll outrun her.
Halfway across the newly plowed garden,
she catches me.
I didn't know mothers could run like that.
Wow!
What a woman!
– *Mary*

Darla Jean

Darla's mother and grandmother
with contented faces
sit peeling apples.
She skips and flits,
as unconcerned as the butterflies
in the nearby meadow.
They explain to us,
in hush-toned voices,
She was so small at birth,
her bed was a cigar box.
They even featured her
in the newspaper.

My eyes focus
on the miracle girl.
Sun halos long blonde curls,
radiant face exuding confidence.
Her ballerina body,
long legs dance by.
She picks up a peeled apple.

Don't you get your hand
slapped for that?

Her father and grandfather
come out of the house, smile at her.

My sister and I
walk home in silence
across the steel bridge,
through the empty fields.
– Mary

Paste and Ingenuity

Mama sits me down in front of a saucer
that holds a bar of soap in a little water.
After demonstrating how it works,
she hands me an empty wooden spool.
I wet one end, suds it up
against the Crystal White,
then blow gently on the dry end
until bubbles fly out.

She teaches Beverly
how to make doll furniture.
Roll back the flaps of Kerr lid boxes,
cover with an old sock ,
fitting them until they resemble
overstuffed couches and chairs.

I am delighted when Mama gives us
the roll end of old wallpaper.
We make paste of flour and water,
cut roses and leaves out of the print,
glue them on paper, and fancy we have
the most beautiful valentines in town.
– Mary

Red

I touch this iron spike
cardinal crusted
flashes of scarlet memory
streaming blood again
from my wound
where, kneeling on a rotted hay wagon
it penetrated just below the knee.

My brother braced his foot against my leg,
pulled with all his might
to wrench the spike free.

Mama screamed
ran inside.

It gushed vermillion. For years,
those images invited residual fear.

Now I hold this ancient nail, wondering
Is my tensile strength as sure
as this nail's core?

I touch the scar.
I needed her.
– *Mary*

The Elberta Players

Daddy was one of the company
that traveled from Elberta
to Mona, Eureka, and some
of the other small towns
putting on plays.
Grandpa Penrod was the director.

Grandpa Keith, Uncle Bill Jolley,
Lavon and Bill were all members
of the troupe.

They put on melodramas like
Tony the Convict,
The Landlord,
and *Where Is My Wandering Boy Tonight?*
Lavon was always the heroine,
Bill, the hero.
– Mary

Once an Actor

The cow is staked in a field
on the other side of the river bridge,
a trestle with steel girders
built over the railroad tracks
that span the Provo River.
I go with Daddy across the bridge
to milk the cow.

A few nights ago, our family
went to watch a play—a melodrama!
The heroine was tied
to the railroad tracks by the villain.
It seemed so real
I cried out loud.

Daddy decides to act out the scene
for me—sets the bucket of milk down
and lays himself across the tracks.
In the distance we hear the train whistle.
His audience of one screams,
pulls at him, jumps up and down, crying.

I guess he is satisfied
that he's still got the stuff—
gets up, picks up his pail,
and laughs all the way home.
– Mary

Grandaddy Trout and the Four-Year Old

My oldest brother knows everything,
explores our world over,
knows the ins and outs,
even the outcrop of the stream ledge
where Grandaddy Trout lives—
enormous, as he shows
wide measure of arms.

When he tells us his plan,
I am one of them.
On the chosen day,
I chase like a devoted pup
after the other three
down the path to the river's edge.

We wade in; Alan gives orders.
Beverly, you stand over there,
Bill, you're next to me.
I guard the rock.

Okay now, be quiet. Don't move.
I hardly breathe. *I'll show them*
they can count on me!
Waiting forever then,
edging out from the dark hole,
a fish nose. He ventures more,
then, sensing boundary of legs,
turns, darts, slices water.

15

They reach and grab.
He swims to me, right into my arms.
I cradle the prize to my chest.
He arches, flaps his tail,
slides easily away,
vanishes, ripple on ripple.
Siblings groan.

Lagging back up the path, I stop,
scuff dust with a determined toe.
I'll never, never let another rainbow
slip from my grasp.
– Mary

Daddy Tucks Me into the Handlebar Basket

He pedals toward town—
a large brick building, lines
and lines of people. I wonder
why no one smiles back.
We wait, edge forward. The man
hands Daddy three brown sealed bags,
packages stored with me for the ride home.
What is it? I ask
Food, he answers.

Curious, on tiptoe I can barely
see the items on the tabletop.
Opened, one reveals rice Mama
pours into in a Mason jar.
The second is flour emptied into the bin.
With the third bag, Mama looks inside,
widens her eyes at me, takes my hand,
and fills it with succulent, wrinkly
raisins. Savoring each one slowly,
I run to find my Dad.

Can we go to that place again tomorrow?

I hope we never do.
– Mary

Billy Keith

Getting yelled at, spanked,
sent to bed without supper
never dampens his recusant smile,
his unflagging good nature.
On this summer day, like many
at the brown house,
Mama is wondering how
she's going to feed her brood of six.
Daddy's gone to Provo to look for work.

Billy's shout brings us to the stoop.
He points under the house.
A white rabbit! A white rabbit!
We often have jackrabbit for a meal,
but we think albino will be a rare treat.
To block the escape of our potential feast
Alan assigns watchers at either outlet.
A lot of shouting, a few sightings,
and suddenly the hare is there,
before Billy and me.
My brother pounces,
comes up with the prize,
but also a piece of wood
with a nail—piercing his hand—
pushing up skin on the top side.

I don't remember dinner,
but I'll never forget the nail print.
– Mary

Alan's in Charge

Our parents have gone
to Provo with Grandpa.
They left the "Model T" at home.

Alan, age twelve, my Daniel Boone,
knows the names of rocks,
can tell us the varieties of lizards,
find ground squirrels, prairie dogs, snakes.

If he'd let me, I'd follow him
on all his excursions.
Today he does.
He includes us kids in on a conspiracy—
he knows how to drive.

We all pile in.
To look grown-up,
Alan puts on Dad's hat.
He takes the gravel road part way,
then wheels out across the sagebrush.
That's when Beverly starts screaming.

We miss ditches; circle haystacks.
He shows us where he finds arrowheads
and how the Indians chipped them from flint.

He puts the car back in its exact spot.
It wasn't us who told on him.
It was Mr. Miller,
wondering why Dad looked so short.
– Mary

18

Grandma's Water Slide

Drought days, dust-filled,
where once grew plentiful orchards,
now a plethora of tumbleweeds,
rows and rows of withered stumps.
Trees and men—sapless—
eke out sustenance
dry-farming our thirsty desert.

Farm folk, sagebrush-hardy,
discover homemade fun.
After chores, Mama hands out gunnysacks.
Seeking relief from parching, we follow
Grandma Penrod, Mrs. Hintze, and Mama,
who hike us up to the Stirling place.
These Easterners have cemented
their irrigation ditch.
The settlement's only concrete waterway
slopes the entire distance of the hill,
slick with slimy moss.

The women with kids lined up
on sacks between their legs,
take turns sitting at the head gate,
ample hips damming the water
until the build-up propels us
flying down the slide.

With wet-washed faces, we soak up fun
like playful otters on a wild ride--
squeal, open-mouthed,
and catch delicious droplets.
Children, like dry seeds swelling,
fill with life.

We climb back up
through dust and rocks
to plunge downward
on another splashing adventure.

A moment's relief on a dreary day
drenches my memory for a lifetime.
– Mary

Lavon's Hands

She flails wet fabric against the washboard with much the
same motion required to punch dough before pinching it
into loaves, stops to rub in lye soap needed to scrub out
brown dirt, as pervasive in summer as snow is in winter.
Mixed in, is the black coal dust Bill brings home from the
silver mines.

She wrings each piece by hand, stirs the boiling starch, and
heats flatirons on the stove, hangs the laundry on the line,
stops, to shake a fist and call to Uncle Harold, who has
the boys captivated under the poplar as he rolls his own.
Stop showing my kids that dirty, awful habit.

She dips the mop in leftover suds, slops it over the plank
floor, then dribbles and smoothes sour cream over the wood.
It dries to a clear stiff shine. She has tidied the house, done
the laundry, fixed a dinner of bread and milk—tonight a
little gooseberry jam to sweeten the bowl.

Before bed, Lavon rubs generous globs of Hollywood
Cold Crème on her red hands. She wants them white and
smooth for church tomorrow to match the ivory keys—like
she was going to play for the Queen of England rather than
our small congregation.
– Mary

When Mama Takes My Hand

Supper dishes done,
Mama takes my hand
for bedtime-outhouse routine.
We pass poplars rustling,
cricket song syncopation
mixing with bass frog notes.
Scent of yellow roses
wraps around us.

Twilight trades crimson
for iris-dark sky
setting off the moon,
already high.
On the walk back,
my steps are slower,
I pull against her hand.
She stops, kneels down,
draws me near,
puts her finger to her lips.

Look.
She points toward the pond
where only this morning
I had toiled
with a tin can,
farming polliwogs.

Giant birds,
coral crested,
great wings drawn down
like cashmere shawls,
come landing, prancing,
bowing, leaping.

They skip, their stick legs
reflecting on the pool
with moon-dance shadows.

I feel my heart tick
as loud as Grandma's clock,
while my eyes gaze amazement.
The scene is mine forever,
when Mama takes my hand.
— Mary

Gray-Blue Galvanized

The day, the sky, and the washtub
are all the same color.
Mama scrubs our clothes on a rutted
washboard, than hangs them out to dry.

Alan brings bucket loads of fresh water
from the irrigation ditch, refills the tub.
Beverly's job is to bring up the Mason jars
from the cobwebbed cellar and make
each one clean enough to hold
peaches for winter eating.

Her nine-year old hand fits
through the small jar mouth.
Kneeling in the dirt before the tub
she scours and rinses each one carefully.

Alan chops kindling, starts a fire
in the wood stove. Mama fills the containers
with fruit she has peeled, puts on the Kerr lids,
submerges them in the canning kettle,
and boils until sanitized and sealed.

Grandpa comes by, gives us a stewing hen.
I help Beverly take the dry clothes from the line,
sprinkle; roll them, so they'll be just right
for ironing tonight. We set the flatiron
on the back of the range to heat.

Alan fills the tub again. This time with water
heated in the reservoir attached to the stove.
Maybe we will fill it twice more
so that everyone, cleanest to dirtiest,
will get a chance to bathe.
Daddy, covered with dust from working
at the Tintic Standard Mine, has to be last.

Tomorrow we'll put fresh clothes
on our clean bodies and go to church.
After church Mama will serve us chicken
and dumplings, homemade bread
and cobbler made from fresh Elberta peaches.
Dad will read scriptures, lead us in family prayer,
thanking God for our abundance.
– Mary

So Happy You Came

We don't have enough money; you can't go.
From Grandma Keith's, the others walk
uptown to the Paramount Theater.
I turn toward home on Fifth South.
Daddy, seeing me, stops in his Ford V 8,
lets me ride home on the running board.
We have something new, he smiles.
What? A dog! A puppy? What?
Shhhhh. Mama smiles, folds down
the blanket—it's love at first sight.
We'll call her Karen;

I lose myself in her soft pinkness.
            Armor from the stings of the world.

Every day after fifth grade,
Venice stands on the corner and talks with me.
Tell me about your little sister.
Gates open; I spill.
She's so smart—
hides her shoes in the flour bin,
remembers where everything is,
picks out notes on the piano,
curly hair, sturdy little legs,
called our calf Mooo.
Stories till dusk.
            Armor from the stings of the world.

Bob and I live in LA while he is in school.
Karen comes to live nearby. We share
cooking, eating, laughing, talking, movies.
Her humor and friendship:
            Armor from the stings of the world.

Needing refuge from every day demands,
I go to Karen's. Her patriarchal blessing
truly tells: She will make her home
a heaven on earth. *Come in, here's a pillow,*
take off your shoes, let's talk,
what can I get you?
Sure, I'll listen to your poem.
            Armor from the stings of the world.
– Mary

Walnut Stains

Daddy sat evenings and cracked defiant
black shells with a ball peen hammer
on a fifty-pound weight. We inhaled

the heady incense, mined treasure
picked from crevices in the shards
until we garnered enough to place on the tongue,
our own musky communion—
taste of autumn mellowing to winter.
The walnut tree stood just east of the house.
As leaves yellowed and shriveled, nuts,
armored in green hulls, hurtled themselves
to the ground. We spread them out to crisp,
stained our fingers with the darkened husks.

Wayne and I sit facing each other
across a stump inside the doorway of the granary
with its hoard of coal and tools.
He pounds the flat edge of Daddy's hatchet
to hammer open the stubborn storehouse
of tawny meat. *You can have this one.*
I reach, eager to smash the nut.
He means to crack it for me,
unaware of the blade.
I scream as blood streams from my hand,
see him shrink back in the shadow of the door,
behind a box. His arms hang limply
at his sides, his eyes dark—a cornered fox.

I don't remember pain, but Wayne
wore it like a burlap pack on his back.

Last year he brought me a quart
of shelled black walnuts to savor.
Penance, he said.
— Helen

Visiting Our Neighbors

Six year-old Donna Coombs, a splinter of a girl, answers
the door, lets me into a room with worn, cracked linoleum,

a table, two chairs, a small stove, bare shelves, and an old trunk. Her father, who resembles Clark Gable, sits on an orange crate between Donna's mother and the mother's sister, both with dyed hair (one black, one red) gelled and clipped in finger waves, their faces expertly painted. All three are smoking Camel cigarettes and sipping coffee diluted to a pale tan with Sego canned milk. Donna tugs at her mother's sleeve, and babbles, coaxing. I strain to understand her strange syllables. Her mother nods, rises—I follow them to the trunk. As the lid is flung back, Donna grins and my hands fly up to cover my mouth. Better than Blackbeard's booty, this chest displays velvets, satins, silks—fringed and trimmed with jewels—and a long-tailed fox fur, head and all.

Her red-headed aunt joins us, gathers a glittering gold garment to her, smiles, and floats the room as she models it and hums *Dancing in the Dark*. To my seven year-old eyes— Ginger Rogers. The mother wipes a tear, takes the wrap, caressingly replaces it, and closes the lid.

Shortly, the family is gone, the trunk abandoned, and then the crumbling stucco demolished. Fifty years later, I drive by the empty lot and still wonder: *Who in the world were the Coombs?*

– Mary

Be Careful What You Say

The words *I'm bored* echoed
through my Mother's house.
Once!

Convinced we will see the *rack*
or some other form of medieval punishment,
the innocent, along with the guilty,

trail after Mama to the front room
with the coal stove, soot-tinted walls.

We stand like soldiers at boot camp,
while she hands each of us a hunk
of wallpaper cleaner,
recites explicit instructions.

The workers clear upholstered furniture
and other obstacles. It takes six of us
to move the upright piano,
although I'd seen Mother move it solo.

We mold, knead, fold, roll the pink stuff
until it resembles a soft rubber ball—
aroma, bubble gum delicious.
At five, I'm an eager participant.
Children varying in height and age
begin their penance. Simon Legree,
minus the whip, supervises.

Youngest children, Karen and Helen,
start from bottom up to tiptoe reach.
Older sisters, Mary Belle and Beverly,
work the middle. Brothers Wayne and Bill,
balance from ladders, their arms making
large swaths up to the ceiling.

Crumbs rain down on workers below,
invade hair, mouths, eyes. I decide
to quit the crew. Simon decides otherwise.
Humming along with the Kirby, we vacuum,
scrub windows, shine mirrors,
straighten bookshelves, and polish furniture
with a sable liquid that stains our hands
like the black walnuts we harvest in fall.

We wash and starch lace curtains,
then stretch them over steel spikes
on large wood frames to dry.

Chores concluded, we examine
our handiwork, smile, sigh satisfaction.

Mama cocks her finger, beckons us outside,
gathers us close while we watch
the sky turn crimson.
– Karen

Dark Dreams About That Day

Alone, I walk the five blocks
to Grandma Keith's house,
down the hill, past Tri-State Lumberyard
with its maze of rough-sawn stacks,
past Z. C. M. I. warehouse,
where that same man stands in the doorway,
then over the train tracks.

There is a wide spot in the Millrace
that flows alongside the avenue—
overgrown on its edges—
privacy from passers-by,
no one around to say no.

I kick off my shoes, wade in,
and ford the chest-high stream.
The acrid rotten-sulfur aroma
hangs the air like the riverwillow
branches overhead.

A sudden sense of danger
impels me up the bank.
Stifling screams, I slap

at my legs and body—
force myself to pluck off leeches
one by one. I examine
every inch, ensure
that I'm free of suckers.

I trudge the remaining
half-block to Grandma's
to play with Aunt Lucille's kids
visiting from Green River.
– Mary

Penrod Reunion at the Hot Pots

The picnic is as yummy as you'd expect
with Grandma's chicken,
Mama's cinnamon rolls
and homemade ice cream.
We eat in a pavilion
with lots of other people.
I only know my own relations,
except for Vera Patton,
whose two sisters look
just like her.

For the program, Bev and I
sing *Mighty Lak a Rose*,
and my aunts, Mary and Lois, sing
It's a Sin to Tell a Lie,
accompanied by Uncle Vern.
Our California cousin,
JoAnn, does tumbling.
But everyone claps hardest
and shouts loudest for Grandpa,
who chords the piano
and sings *The Old Maid*,
and *The Cat Came Back*.

Most amazing to me
are the hot pots.
My cousins and I scramble
up the sides of these huge
mineral-crusted cones. I stop
to see a butterfly, dry and papery
clinging to a scraggle of thistle.
On the lip we peer
at the bubbling mud inside.
It looks like fudge we boil
on our Monarch stove.

Mama lets me rent a bathing suit.
It's gray and too big.
I'm embarrassed and afraid,
but not enough to stay out of the pool.
I brave it alone.
Out of the chlorine-smelling deep,
Alan appears and takes me in his arms.
We paddle to where the water is over my head.
He says, *Sink or swim!* and lets me go.

I sink
and think
butterflies are still beautiful,
even after they're dead.
– Mary

Evening Echoes

I don't know anymore
where the railroad tracks lie.
Or when the trains run.
But I hear the whistle
across the miles of the night.
How close it seems.
I knew where the tracks were

when we grew up just a block away—
on this side.

Chores slacken; games take full steam.
Jaunty voices shout the evensong,
train's whistle blends with the descant
of mothers' voices: suppertime calls
toss around the neighborhood,
bouncing over the houses,
over the rooftops,
like Auntie-Eye-Over balls that ricochet,
gable-to-gable, chimney to chimney,
finally arching out of sight.

BILL-eee, Bill-eeEE!
Oh, B-O-eeyd. Donnie JO-o-oe.
Way-AYne, Mary BELLE!
JIM-eee, Jim-eeEE, JIM-MEEE!
When Jimmy Perry's mom got
that certain ring to her voice,
he'd run without looking back like Lot,
when his wife turned to salt.

Now and then at night
sleep stammers, waking wanes.
I hear a train from far away
calling through my dreams,
edging the backyard of my
memory space,
shaking loose the echoes of those voices.
– Helen

It's a Tradition

We have waited till the Fourth of July
for the first picking.
Pick faster, Wayne.

It's getting dark and Mama's
Wearever aluminum mixing pan
is only half-full.

Daddy has set the ladder
against the rear of the house.
We scramble up like squirrels with treasure.
On the flat part of the roof we spread
a heavy old quilt we've dragged up—
the patchwork that covers the boys
when they sleep on the unheated porch
in winter.

From here we see through open sky
above Daddy's nursery trees,
all the way from Fifth South to the stadium.
I cuddle Helen and Karen to me,
and set the pan between Wayne and us.
Snapping open my first firm, full pod,
I run my finger down its spine,
and pop the tender balls into my mouth,
sweeter even than I remembered.

This is better than hundred-dollar seats.
I hope the fireworks are as good as the peas.
– Mary

Pendulum

Summer stretched forever when
I was young, days even longer.
Yellow days hanging on the hem of yellow days
invite me, coax me to escape from Mother's
endless list of chores, past the vacant lot
to Craven's corner and the ditch bank.

Before cement, dark earth coffined
deep flowing water, edged by overgrown
weeds and pink hollyhocks,
tall enough for shade,
thick enough for hiding.

Safe and sheltered, I gently pull
long tender shoots for nibbling,
pick buttercups bunched with bachelor's buttons
to crown the cucumber boat and me.

Stomach down,
I try to catch triple-decker skeeters,
dancing, darting,
defying my small hands
and the matchbox jail.

I was there again this morning,
wrapped in soft sheets,
snuggled in warm blanket memories.
Awakened senses recall the smell of wet earth,
the scent of yellow petals in my hands,
halos in my hair.

Amazing, fifty years have gone more quickly
than those afternoons
when I was six or five or seven.

– Karen

Runaway

I'm eleven.

I put five year-old Karen on the bike's back fender, eager
to give her a ride. We go only a few yards—she falls off,
cries. Babysitter Alan sees the whole thing. *You dummy!* He
thumps me on the head, gives me a push.

That's it.

I start walking—*I'm not staying here*. Adrenaline propels me down the dip, up the hill. It's dark when I turn south at Springville Road, still walking fast. Almost past Springville I turn down a rural road, find a secluded place among the cattails.

This might be a good place to sleep. Instead, I retrace steps to Main Street and the city park. Kids are playing on the swings. We talk—I tell them I'm going to my aunt's house. I'm swinging when the kids' parents pick them up. A few minutes later, a police car pulls up; two policemen question me, tell me, *You're not going to make it to your aunt's tonight. Let us take you home*.

My parents, relatives, and siblings, are all on the front lawn when we arrive. I'm struck that they have been concerned about me. I don't get a spanking. Mama never sat on the edge of my bed before. She does now, doesn't speak, but strokes my hair and forehead until I fall asleep.

– *Mary*

Pressed Petals
for Rita

After you arrive from Omaha,
we begin the business
of becoming *Frog and Toad*.
Together, hopping and skipping blossom-time,
your spring-coiled ringlets trampolining,
we explore our four-block world.

Neighborhood children don't ring doorbells
or knock on doors; so from lawns and porches,
in *profundo* voices, we call: *Ree-ta, Ka-ren*.

Summer is spent in Johnsons' backyard hand-fishing
in minnow-filled water until our skin ruffles.
Steps away, an outhouse accommodates:
weathered brown planks,
two seats, bottom-sanded smooth.

Rita and I fly to George's store
to spend my wartime nickel knotted
in a handkerchief, pinned in my pocket
to insure its safety. We buy a popsicle.

Below the railroad tracks where hobos
live in boxcars, the jungle beckons.
We listen for Tarzan's swinging-vine cry,
watch for Johnny through shadowed trees.
Like ballerinas, the two of us tiptoe
along the rails, arms waving balance,
head to the forbidden ice plant,
shiver through rooms of lockers stuffed with meat.

Siamese-connected, we zigzag the empty lot,
dart across Third South,
kick leaves all the way to Kindergarten.

Like Dorothy in Oz, Penny plops from the sky,
lands next door to you. Two become three,
arms linked in forever.

Kneeling on the couch, curtains pulled aside,
I watch them play, hear their echoes.
Pen-nee, Ree-ta.

We still go to the same schools after you move,
say *Hi* in halls as long as years.
Bound now to others, the past is pressed
and put away like fragile petals.

At Mother's funeral,
fragrance of blossoms dancing air,
we hug away four decades of separation.

Did you hear me calling?
– Karen

Bring Your Own Salt Shaker

The rhubarb is high, the stalks crisp.
Their variegated scarlet and green skins
tell us it's time.

My brothers Billy and Wayne,
George and Ken Collard,
Jimmy Perry and Jolene join me
at the end of our lot against Bandley's fence.

We burrow,
half hidden beneath the Concord vines,
within pluck of the puckery stalks.
With skill, you can snap the end and peel
the outer membrane off in one-piece strips.

Billy passes me the red and white
Woolworth shaker. Enough salt
makes the tart taste palatable—
even delectable.

Now we're ready for the scary sharing of stories:
the wandering departed,
searching for lost limbs,
girls who haunt the highways,
the white lady in the forest,
the girl in a formal trying to get to the prom,
footsteps in the attic…

We've ingested just about as much fear
and acidity as we can hold,
when the mothers' insistent calls beckon.

One by one we break the cloister
with the promise of another gathering,
more torturous tales—
and don't forget your shaker.
– Mary

She Reads To Me

Five days into first grade,
rheumatic pain circles my body,
settles in legs curled in distress.
My illness lingers through seasons of tinted trees,
white frost and seedtime, then I return
like a new leaf for the last days of learning.

Throughout this time, my older sister, Helen,
gathers lessons from Mrs. Hanson,
brings them home, and we play school.
She shows me how to match images
in my workbook, to write and spell small words.
Arithmetic, easier to spell than do,
means adding numbers, taking them away
until our fingers disappear.

Snuggled together in the overstuffed chair,
we scan a book full of pictures.
Dick commands, *Look, Jane, look.*
Jane looks and says, *See Spot run,*
as she points to a black-and-white-dotted dog
chasing balls across the pages.

Weary from work, I rest against my teacher
while she reads to me from Daddy's grade school primer

about a little French girl, Cosette.

A greedy couple receives money to care for her,
but treat her as a servant. Even on Christmas Eve,
sky buried in black, they send her to get water
from the spring. Bending over the freezing runnel,
hands wrapped around the bowed handle,
she baptizes the bucket, sloshing cold
down her apron and naked knees.
She sighs deep grown-up sighs,
her life heavy as the water.

Then a stranger comes, carries her burden.
At the tavern where Cosette lives,
the gentle man watches her knitting stockings
for the couple's children, her own feet bare
and winter blue. At bedtime, still young enough
to believe in goodness, she places her tiny
wooden shoe next to the useless fireplace.
On Christ's morning, hidden in her hope,
a gold Louis, and beside her shoe,
that most beautiful doll in the world,
the one she had gazed at every time
she went for water—a child starved for beauty,
hungry to hold it to her heart.

Every day we visit our friend, cry for her.
How lonely our days become when the book
she lives in, disappears. Years later,
like a resurrection, we find her in the middle
of *Les Miserables*. Its thickness unburdens
decades of anxiety as we read that her rescuer,
Jean Valjean, became a father to her,
sheltered and cared for her, loved her,
and taught eight-year-old Cosette to read.
My sister, Helen, just eight-years-old, taught me.
– Karen

Eight Loaves

I imagine I can smell it when I reach
the vacant lot, float on the aroma
down the path, past Strong's,
through the back door, into the kitchen.
Mother cuts the coveted heel,
spreads it Grandma Knighton style:
scrape off more than you put on.
Then, ceremoniously, she places
the prize in my hands.

No one can duplicate the bread.
I know why. One morning as the ritual began,
I meticulously took notes,
watched every move, counted the stirs,
clicked a mental picture to pattern.
Depression-conscious,
she added leftover mush,
mixed it with the other ingredients
as though it belonged.

She kneaded like a champion boxer
taking on his punching bag
with perfect rhythm, well-trained arms.
Baking was the clincher:
coal stove, blackened pans.

I miss the bread.
I miss the constancy of it,
its goodness, its healing power.

How could she have known as she
went about her mundane chore
what it would mean to us,

her eight loaves of delicious children,
stirred, kneaded and baked, who
live the legacy of Mama's bread.
– *Karen*

Alan Turns Eighteen

First of eight children,
he startles in his élan,
in the grace of his going,
in tender attention to little sisters.
From my ten years' distance
he seems a man,
carries himself tall,
shoulders rivaling Atlas.

My brothers all run,
pole vault, high jump,
like our Dad,
who erects pole-vaulting standards
at the foot of the garden,
softens the pit with sawdust,
from somewhere finds a bamboo pole.

Alan leads the way.
Right in the middle of the garden
in the middle of the war,
he turns eighteen.
They draft him, send him. . . where?
We search the map, find Amarillo
in the top hat of Texas. Crowding
the round kitchen table, we wait for Mama,
who smoothes out pages of his letters
on the faded roses of the oilcloth cover.
I grasp and hold each word.

Propped against our treasured pump organ,
I reread his letters.
Sun stares through the big window,
refracting rainbows from
the jewels and beveled glass
that prism onto the pages.
Each letter written so beautifully,
the words have wings to take flight
into the shattered light.

He writes poems to the family.
One night Mama
sets a page in front of me,
irons it with her hand.
Her mouth puckers
like she is tasting tart cherries.

> *To Helen*
>
> With shyest modesty surrounding
> Every action, light and airy
> Of her trim stature, so like a fairy.
> Her sweetest voice with song abounding
> Calls my dreamy thoughts to tarry
> While I listen to her merry
> Tuneful laughter still resounding.
> --J. Alan Keith

His words shine through the prism of my heart.

Each night Mother sits on my bed;
we pray for Heavenly Father
to help me be a good girl,
bless children in war-torn countries,
bless Alan and keep him safe.
Just before his battalion ships out,
he catches pneumonia,

is confined to hospital.
I know God has heard my prayers.

Snow melts; buds open their fists.
I relish burnished air as I walk from school--
two blocks from home,
I think I glimpse a uniform.
Steps and heart quicken.
My head feels like a balloon
lifting up in the breeze.
My lips form words:
> *Oh, Heavenly Father, please, let it be Alan.*
> *Please let it be Alan. Please, please, please.*

I turn up our walk, he leaps off the porch,
swings me in a bear hug. His molasses laughter
sweetens my spirit.

I think of him now, big brother,
pouring rich tones,
ringing bright notes of our singing days
soothing the going of our years,
balming the reasons for our tears.
> *Thank you, thank you, thank you.*

– Helen

Land Of Milk And Music

Mary, like the rest of us,
never knew the cow's *real* name.
We only heard it addressed
in expletives from Dad's mouth.
Politically-savvy, she also denied
its existence when with friends,
she saw it strolling down Main Street,
rope dangling from neck,
full udder swinging free.

At get-togethers, before the singing,
cow stories begin, brothers embellish
recollections: who milked, who fed,
who *held the cow out*
more than the others.

Cow time for me, a girl of seven,
consisted of social calls
while ol' what's-her-name was tethered
at the back of our lot awaiting transfer
to Aunt Pearl's grassy pasture.

That cow concluded the reign,
the fifth and the last to bear
the family moniker,
That Damned-Hell-fired-Damn-Cow!

Our fourth cow, same name,
remains the most memorable.
Dad fed and milked her twice a day
as faithfully as the sun and moon rise.
She produced buckets of rich milk
that Mother strained through
a flour-sack-turned-dish towel,
filling a squatty round enamel-coated pan
that doubled for making bread.

Mama skimmed rich clumpy cream
for butter, for topping cereal
and made-from-scratch desserts.
With part of the remaining milk,
she made large curd Dutch cheese,
stored the rest in our ancient icebox
in a corner on the back porch.

Mama strained the afternoon batch,
poured the warm foamy milk
into tin pails with large bowed handles,

cream already peaking.
Then the milkman, eight-year-old Wayne,
carried two containers to Williams Music Store,
delivered it to the owners
living in the rear of the converted house.
In return, they brought to us
an upright mahogany piano.

How many milkings,
how many strainings,
how many trips?

It was years before I realized we were poor,
only rich people owned pianos
and cows.
– *Karen*

The Cellar

In a different century,
certainly a different millennium,
our cellar would have been labeled a dungeon.

A cramped window filtered light
through years of neglect.
Out of short people's reach,
a 25-watt bulb dangled
three steps into dreaded dark.

Steep cement steps, like the ones my older
brother Alan rode his tricycle down,
led to slanted shelves stacked
with canned recollections.

Barren bottles, home for stringy
sticky threads, incubated unrivaled

varieties of spiders. Later, an eight-armed
octopus occupied the cellar's last space,
gushing heat into a cold house.

Taunted,
I dared to face the black widows
and the dark. My eyes squinted
to retrieve the day's supply
of preserved bounty. I chose peaches—
everybody's favorite, except for Mama
who was partial to summer apricots—
carried the offering in a two-quart Mason jar
to siblings swallowing seconds of hot bread.

Sometimes when it rains,
like today, I smell the dank cellar,
walk down the steps again,
retrieve my bottled memories.
– Karen

The Crooner

The old coal stove cools
as summer turns to evening.
Billy leaps up, making it his stage,
grabs the dangling light bulb
and croons into it.
His chestnut curls
wisp against his forehead,
just like Frankie's.
Beverly, Karen, and Mary
squeal and swoon.
Frank takes second place for sisters.
– Helen

February Lesson

Second grade.
The most wonderful teacher in the world,
Rosalind Russell and Eleanor Roosevelt in one.
Until that day in February.

Excitement to create ripples around me.
Such lovely things, unexpected
in this wartime world:
red, white, and pink crepe paper,
construction paper, scissors, paste.
Even paper lace doilies!

Rex sits across the aisle and back one seat,
uncombed, unwashed,
legs cramped under the too-small desk.
They came last year, those who work
for the railroad, living in boxcars
beside the tracks. Kids call him dumb
with his thick glasses and ragged socks.

Children are caught up in creating.
Thundering, Mrs. Krell looms over him,
hands on hips,
Whoever told you pink and red go together!
My heart catches, hesitates.
I barely breathe.
Her words erase joy.
He can't read, can't do arithmetic.
There is nothing he does well.
It doesn't matter with a valentine.

At seven, I learned a February lesson,
circling in red ink that child's moment,
cutting out hearts in second grade.
– Helen

Eating Tomatoes With My Brother

I'd like to return with you
to that backyard garden,
stretching clear back
to Bandley's fence.

Armed with a salt shaker,
we take two, maybe three,
red succulent tomato bulbs
bigger than one hand can hold,
sit on fertile earth
between sheltering rows of corn
grown twice as high as I.

We salt and bite,
salt and bite, slurp the juice
before it can run down,
dripping seeds on my pinafore
or your tee shirt.

And this time Mama
wouldn't need to be mad.
There would be no willow cut
for you, no butter paddle for me.

We would all sit together
shaded by the black walnut tree,
hear breezes sweep the leaves,
birds shuffle their feathers,
while we shell peas.

– Helen

Back Porch Trunk

My daughters came Halloween-hunting:
costumes for their children. A blouse for one,
Grandpa's letterman sweater for another.

If only I had the trunk,
the one tightly packed for emergency voyages,
reeking with moth balls, mixed
with the forgotten, pungent even
through the thick and padded years.

Overflowing with coats, skirts, capes,
scarves, winter quilts—all used,
stored, used again, their lives longer
than the lives of those who claimed them.

When necessity arose, small shadows,
sensing ceremony, marched behind Mama,
circled the silent wringer washer,
skirted cellar steps, stopped at the trunk.

During one excursion, Beverly found
a pair of long johns among the treasures,
dyed them black, painted florescent bones,
making them dance in a moonless sky,
then returned them to the trunk.

Twelve-year-old Wayne found a shirt,
brand new, just his size.
No one remembered seeing it before.
New! Not leftover from older brothers.
Brand new.

When I was princess of the second grade circus,
Mama dug through the cast-offs,
uncovered a yellow-dotted tulle dress

Aunt Doree had worn at sixteen,
remodeled it back to life.

It had capped puffy sleeves, fitted to the waist,
gathered, tied with a sash. The skirt dropped
to the floor, making my feet twirl.

Last Halloween, disguised in stale
reminiscence, I danced the yellow dress again,
whirled through the tunnel toward the past,
trick-'n-treated myself.

– Karen

Stringing Beads

My first best friend and I searched
for treasure behind her house.
Where rain dripped from eaves,
we found tiny rocks glinting in sunlight,
pieces of colored glass: rubies, emeralds,
diamonds—and bugs we held like jewels
as they rolled themselves up into beads.

I see a dragonfly darting, darning
holes in my sky, stitching together
prayers and songs I sang as a child,
stringing them, knotting the ends:
pearls to present to God.

I sat with my daughter, guiding
the dull needle as she strung popcorn.
She sits with her daughters threading
jewels of colored glass, boxes of rainbows.

Blackbirds, strung like onyx beads
on the power line, lift together
and scatter, the necklace breaking.

I look for pieces under my bed,
in the corners. Fingers brush
back and forth, so I don't miss
what I cannot see.

My husband recounts stories
nospaceinbetween, linked
like paper chains on a Christmas tree
until they connect ending to beginning.

This morning he brought me
a dead dragonfly, arms folded,
wings wide to span a lifetime.
I frame it against a sky, watch,
wait for the signal to unfold,
to wing our way home
– Helen

My Englishman

George Ramsbotham—white as the flour he hoarded in the back room of his tiny store, white as the starch in his stiff collar; white as the butcher's apron wrapped twice around him, white as the few hairs haloing his shiny bald head emitting more light than the single pale bulb at the end of the dangling cord—

left his homeland with his wife Elizabeth, while war was full bloom, planted seeds in foreign Utah soil. He talked different, had a strange name, a wife but no children.

At five, a world away from bombs, war meant the star in our front window signified Alan was a soldier. We needed ration stamps for rationed food, and I had to eat everything on my plate because there were hungry children   somewhere.

George opened his grocery store in our neighborhood. I dreaded the two-block trek, dragging the dilapidated wagon, because the never-smiling Mister Ramsbotham terrified me.

I pushed Mother's list of necessities across the slick wood counter he brought from Liverpool, the counter that separated our worlds. Sitting on the chair wedged between the freezer and wall, I watched while he shuffled around the converted breakfast nook with his stepstool, retrieved soda crackers, buckwheat flour, rolled oats, and corn meal from ceiling-high shelves, white margarine from the glass-front cooler. He meticulously listed each item on the charge pad, calculating figures in his head.

Sometimes, like a magician pulling rabbits from hats, he pulled from under his apron, white sugar, raisins, two or three eggs, a banana for Mama. For Daddy, Christmas oranges and hard-tack candy to hide in children's stockings. George buried the riches under groceries in the bottom of a brown paper bag, scarcities squirreled away for a family of nine.

After George died, Elizabeth sold the counter to buy a casket. Max bought it, saw beneath its facade when the rest of us did not. He stripped layers of varnish, sanded the surface smooth, polished until the scarlet grain of cherry wood emerged.

Years erase the layers of my not knowing. I see it now, emanating beauty like the soul of the man who stood behind it.

– Karen

Gently Turned

Eager children watch through breath-frosted
windows for the tree. Its arrival welcomes the season.

There it stands, naked and shivering
in the middle of the room
dispensing intoxicating aroma—
a cedar, cut forty miles away on Grandpa's land.
An ugly tree, we think, not real to us,
color more like sage than evergreen.
We walk round and round this symbol,
see thirsty limbs turned brown from want,
sparse growth, branches broken.
We feign excitement, masking disappointment.

Unaware of little ones with shattered
expectations, Mom and Dad begin
to move the tree. Try over here, the corner next.
Turn it halfway to show the good side,
back a little, turn once more.
Pull, push, adjust, balance.

Satisfied, Mama wraps the lights,
places child-crafted keepsakes, and ornaments.
Wrinkled icicles, smoothed, hung one by one
bring to life each blessed bough.
Fuzzy-suited Santa, cut from coloring book cover,
fills the hole in front and on top,
robed in spun glass, an angel.

In awe, we watch this transformation.
Miracle complete,
a humble tree glories in becoming.

Children, when gently turned just right—
best side showing, wrapped carefully in brightness,

trimmed with ornaments of gratitude,
kissed by the whisper of angel's breath,
then, like trees for Christ—they too, become.
– *Karen*

Daddy Can Really Kick

Always trying to better his score
he uses the top of the door jamb
as his measure.
He's doing well tonight.
One last kick…

Wayne is on his way to bed
with a heated flat iron
wrapped in a dish towel
as a promise of warm feet
in the cold front bedroom.

Dad's foot and the iron connect
at the precise moment Wayne passes.
I see it arc in slow motion and sail
all the way across the living room
like a paper airplane. I don't think
about the pain or the smashed vase
at the other end of the room.

But, boy, Daddy can really kick!
– *Mary*

A Ride to Grandma's

I feel a poem haunting
like wind smacking
the back screen door

half off its hinges,
clapping for attention.

Wind whips to me
across alkaline flats
making eddies around
a patch of sagebrush,
gives up, moves on.

That stretch of road
between Santaquin and Goshen
flaunts its lark that sits,
toes splayed atop a cedar post,
its trill coming just after we pass.
The barbed wire sags in rusty scallops.

I watch with five or six siblings
piled like kittens in the back seat.
Mary begins the chant,

I can se-ee Grandma's house. . .
The others join in,

but all I see are the watery waves
that puddle and float on the road
just out of reach
of the old green Buick.
– Helen

When Mama Laughed

The sepia photograph shows her
in her broad-brimmed hat
net wrapped around the crown
framing her laughing face.

Bertha sits behind Mama
clutching onto the sled;
folding giggles into her shoulder.
Mama's ankle-length dress,
pushed up by her knees,
reveals bloomers. Wind flaps her coat.

That is not the mother I remember.
I see her wearing worry, stretching money
thin as heels of worn out socks to feed
a family of nine. Sighing through Saturdays,
the weight of work presses us down--
we can never get it all done.

One day she comes
around behind the house,
knuckles pressed
into a soundless mouth,
holding in sobs like Mary Pickford
in the silent movies.
I know there is no place for her to run,
no one to bandage her heart.

One night Bess and Jess come by.
We circle the chairs to play
Peter, James and John
and *This Is a Cat; This Is a Dog.*
Her laughter bubbles up,
bringing tears to her eyes,
ringing light into my bones,
filling my hunger better than bread.

– Helen

Sssssafety First

Elberta has no shortage of snakes.
We stay away from blow snakes,
play with garden snakes,
and swim in the canal with water snakes.

A few days ago, Uncle Bill
came home with a set of rattles
he had extracted from a rattlesnake.
He explained that each segment
represented one year in the viper's life.

Jean and I are playing in Grandma's yard.

Oh look, that rattler is heading
straight for the well.

We better stop him.

We better save the drinking water.

I pick up a large rock, hit
the reptile on the head.
He just lies there.

Quick, let's bury him.

We gather every rock we can find,
add one on one until he's completely covered.
We have a considerable altar of stone.

How many sections did his rattles have?

I don't know, he was pretty old.
Eight or nine, maybe fifteen!

We better pull 'em off.

The serpent slithers out from under his grave
and S's out of sight.

Hey, he got away.

Yeah, lucky for him.
– Mary

Happy Trails

My eyes are open
long before dawn pinks—
before the rooster crows reveille.
Come on, Jean.
We throw on our clothes,
clomp down the narrow plank stairs,
burst into the yard, full of anticipation.
At least, I do.
Jean rides horses every day—
no new adventure for her,
but I can always infect her
with my wild spirit.

My uncles lead Pinto and Snake Eyes
to where we wait on the dewy grass.
They help us mount:
We swing short legs over wide girth.
They cinch the saddle, adjust the stirrups,
hand me the reins, *For right, pull right,*
smile at my enthusiasm.
The porch screen bangs and Grandma
hurries over to hand us up large hot biscuits
slathered in butter—
butter I helped churn yesterday,

57

dripping with honey from Grandpa's bees,
and topped with thick crispy bacon.

Jean, in charge now,
heads out across sagebrush flats.
Watch out for rabbit holes.
Let's lope, follow me.
We slow to a walk.
Okay now, Gene Autry is my boyfriend;
Roy Rogers can be yours.
We sing, voices big as sky:
Home on the Range, Wagon Wheels, Cool Water,
Yippee Ki Yi Ai, Tumblin' Tumbleweeds,
snatches of each, repeating over and over
the lines that we know.
By the time we get to *I'm an Old Cowhand,*
leather is boring into bone.
All day plans abbreviate.
It will be some time
before *I'm back in the saddle again.*
– Mary

Taking My Cue From Shirley Temple

Dad talks about Mrs. Binks in glowing terms; Mom,
with nagging bitterness. Dad got hired at Geneva, the
new steel mill, where Mrs. Binks is a secretary. Dad feels
blessed to have a job that pays on the national scale after
the Depression. His job is in the chemical plant where he
separates elements from ore and refines its byproducts. His
lunch bucket always smells of benzol and his conversation
of Mrs. Binks.

In my bones, I know that Dad's integrity is intact. I'm with
him when we run into her at Woolworth's. She has dyed
black hair and red lipstick, is friendly and warm, and at the
same time loud, like Aunt Doree.

Mom decides to go deer hunting with Dad. I think it is because of her. They leave me in Elberta with Aunt Lynn and Uncle Walt—Alan says he can baby sit better if I am not there. After the hunt on the drive home, Mom begins haranguing. I decide to rescue the situation like Shirley Temple when she stood between her movie parents and sang. So from the back seat of the Model T, I sing:

> I wouldn't take a million
> for a Mom and Dad like you,
> I wouldn't take a million
> for the million things you do…

I can't remember the rest of the song, so I just keep repeating the same two lines over and over. It works for me like it did for Shirley.
Peace the rest of the way home.
– Mary

Beverly and Max

She taught me astronomy
of the movie stars,
how to raise one eyebrow,
how colors complement and clash.

I remember her singing
He shall feed his flock like a she-epherd…,
and My sister and I remember, still….

I saw her enchanting young men
with her auburn-framed laughter
as they met coming and going.

She involved us all, weaving fantasy
for the college prom with cellophane,

crepe paper and wire--
flowers tall enough to vault reality.

He comes
with his polished-walnut voice
intoning Shakespeare and Shaw,
making us weep for *La Boheme*
as we see it through his Marcello's eyes.
The Corn Is Green for these two.

He brings liver sausage sandwiches,
Bavarian Mengué,
poetry rich with metaphor into our lives.

Then the conversation of one,
either one,
winds down the years.
Death catches him up
in mid-poem at the computer.

I see her now,
through chiffon-draped windows,
wandering among the fragments,
artifacts of memories, reflected
in blue and rose and gold of carnival glass,

rewriting her book of poetry,
and rewriting,
washing, waiting,
and washing and watching,
caught in the revolving door
of her life.
   - Helen

Summer Events

Alan and Maxine had their first baby
the end of May—a little boy named Jay.
Bill and Colleen would be married in August;
Beverly and Max planned a September wedding.
Mother was expecting her eighth child
late in July—after a ten-year hiatus.
The rest of us walked on eggs.

This advent? I was stunned.
Mama didn't talk to me
the way other mothers talked
to twelve year-old daughters.
Everyone at church knew
she was pregnant before I did.
It was as though everyone knew
Christmas was tomorrow—except me.
She was a little overweight,
and I didn't expect such a thing.
Neither did she.

The sisters start calling the baby Kathleen,
after Daddy's favorite double-cousin.
We don't consider a boy.
Alan takes her for a bumpy ride
in the mountains to hurry things up.
It didn't.
Karen was sent away
to stay with our cousin Nancy.
She hadn't known either.

Morning, July 26—
Mary, Wayne, and I float
like helium balloons
bumping the ceiling and each other,
waiting for Dad to deliver the news.

He pulls into the drive,
gets out, surveys the yard,
picks up a scrap here, a weed there—
deliberately slowing down time.
We are breathless,
burst through the open door
to meet him,
don't believe when he grins,

It's a boy!

They name him Lon
after Daddy's double-cousin—
Kathleen's brother.
He becomes the center of the Keith family universe.
– Helen

I Don't Need to Remember

how mad Mama was at me
for washing my new velvet bonnet
in the well, or how everyone pointed
and laughed at me after I shed my clothes
and wandered naked down the lane.

I don't need to remember
that I caught chicken pox from my sister
because I sucked on her jawbreaker
after she set it down,

or being shunned by Mable and Dave
because I broke the ceramic dog
that sat on their coffee table.

What I will remember are hours of discovery
with my cousin Jean, exploring ghost houses
and finding treasure—

a chipped teacup, a curled shoe,
cactus blooming red and yellow amidst
a paucity of snow, taking a bar of soap along
when we went skinny-dipping in the canal,
an owl silhouetted against the sunset,
and Grandpa's laugh that wheezed out
like the release of air from an accordion
when he and his boys traded stories by lamplight
around the kitchen table.

I'll remember grown-ups coaxing me to sing,
and I'll sing.
– Mary

Mulligan Music

1
Graveyard shift sends Daddy home
with the sun, his body aching for rest.
Lying flat, he stretches muscled arms wide
across the double bed, inviting children—
two, sometimes three to an arm—
to snuggle in for a sing-a-long.
Dad's rich baritone leads with his signature song,
Carolina Moon. Peggy O'Neil is next,
Grandpa Penrod's parody tacked on the end.
Today, a new one, *Stumblin' All Around*;
it becomes our favorite forever.

2
At the kitchen sink, stuck in the corner
by the back door, sisters remove traces
of evening meal, an alto, two sopranos
and me. Rounds go with dish-doing:
Hi Ho, White Coral Bells, even
Three Blind Mice. Brothers, two basses

and a tenor, walk through on their way
to somewhere, join in, creating a choir.
We sing until the kitchen shines.

3

The piano resides in a cubby off the living room,
a niche just big enough for our huge upright.
I call it the sunroom. Rainbow prisms
slice through leaded glass windows,
splash walls with kaleidoscope patterns.
Mom's inside garden decorates:
red geraniums potted in terra-cotta.
Feathery ferns in tandem with philodendrons
drape bare glass. Mama whirls the stool to high,
stretches her short legs to reach pedals,
plays sheet music for her seed to sing:
What's the Good Word Mr. Bluebird,
Johnny Zero and *Old Man River,*
wartime treasures bought without ration stamps.

4

Years blow away our youth like dandelion fluff,
siblings leave, trek their paths, then circle back
to the music house on 5th South, walls swell
to accommodate in-laws, babies,
and Uncle Vern. He claims the piano stool;
stays and plays to fill our cups. Vern's mind
collects music like a miser hoards money,
music he hears but dim eyes cannot see.
Thousands of melodies are rescued
from thought, flow to black and white.

5

Vern is eighty-seven now, still plays
for sing-a-longs. Friends, joining
with family remnants, gather together,
dredge from sagging memories *our* songs,

Gershwin, Foster, Cohan . . . songs
so dear we peel them from places
fastened on our hearts.
And, if we listen carefully, we hear
Bill and LaVon singing, their song ringing
through time, whispering their hope.
– *Karen*

After Ten Vacant Years

my baby brother is born,
his coming like sugar on top of bread and milk,
his delivery (even more revered than Jumbo's
baby-boy-elephant dropped from the sky
filling the void in his mother's barren breast).

A half-century spent between then and now
leaves me longing to see his growing again,
so sometimes I squint real hard,
conjure up glimpses of those evaporating
sugar-sprinkled years.

When he's three, regular as reveille,
he agitates tired siblings and parents awake
by playing his only 45 record over and over
and over and over—Hopalong Cassidy
singing Horace The Horse.

When he's thirteen, he still plays his 45's,
but now his collection includes:
The Four Freshman, Dave Brubeck,
Nat King Cole, and Stan Kenton.
That's when we become friends.

Eyes almost closed, I see him walking home
from Farrer Jr. High lugging his cello

to Mr. Hilgendorf's for lessons,
or stopping by my apartment just to visit.

Fast forwarding, I replay on the fading screen
the last seconds of the championship football
game when he quarterbacked my husband's
high school team. Lonnie cocks his arm,
searches the field for a receiver, aims the ball,
throws the perfect winning pass.

When he's twenty-one
we begin our Thanksgiving traditions—
Rook and swimming. He comes to my home
in Idaho with Mom and Dad,
bringing Pat who is soon to become his wife.
Each year they return with their newest addition:
Emilee, Jennifer, Jeremy . . .

until there are nine.

Sliding down another decade finds Lon and Pat
playing Charades and Pictionary
with my long-distance married children,
laughing away light-hearted moments.

Now he's two again. Sweet reflections
douse me in delight. I call his name
down that long corridor and he runs to me,
blonde curls bouncing, his smile beaming my past.

My little brother, even holding a feather in his fist,
can't fly like the famous Dumbo,
but with Pat at his side, he soars.

    – Karen

May I Have This Dance?

Gentle breeze teases leaves to drop.
I am trying to take in the masses of fall color.
From the canyon pavilion the jukebox blares.
He purposefully approaches the machine,
puts in his quarter,
turns to me, offering his hand.

But I don't waltz. Put on some jazz or swing.

I'll teach you; it's easy.

Step, step, close; step, step, close; step, step close.
Strauss is compelling.
My partner, strong, his steps exact.
He turns as he patterns.
Soon we are circling the redwood deck, whirling.

I throw my head back, laughing.
I am Anna with the King,
Eliza Doolittle at the ball.
We are dandelion down on the wind
with the Vienna Woods keeping us afloat.

Caught in the swirl, a blur with the leaves,
green to flame, gold to bronze, lemon
to raspberry. Soon the delicious cotillion
is over—sadly, never another.
I am nineteen
and he is my Dad.

– Mary

January's Cold

The neighbor's winding driveway
makes a perfect track for eight-year-olds
and Christmas sleds; sleds branded across
the smooth top in bold red letters, *Flexible Flyer*.

The boys sail the air. lean their bodies to make the curve,
steer the stretch, then last minute, swerve,
crash-stop against the snowbank.
Only Jay doesn't stop,
instead he zooms onto the icy road.

Car, sleigh and body intersect slow motion,
wood slivers float the dusky sky.
Shattered symbols bleed scarlet
on fresh snow.

Jay's at the hospital
before my brother Alan hears the news.
At Emergency, he finds his wife, finds his son—
too late to say good-bye to.

Outside, the ruby-rimmed dying sky
hides winter's frail sun. Cold seeps through
to grieving parents, icing the path
from barren cubicle to waiting room.

They see the young driver of the car braced
against the wall, hands gripped across his chest.
Alan pauses, wraps his arms around the boy
and whispers, *Everything will be all right*.

At the cemetery, my father and brothers
place the small coffin on January's frozen ground.
Wind circling headstones penetrates my thick wool coat,
burrows through skin and bones,
slithers next to my pain.

– Karen

Lon Grew Up

thinking he was as old
as his siblings. He and I talk.
His kindergarten friend walks
with leg braces. Lon watches
him go all the way across
the tricky-bars, cheers him on.
The other kids pull faces, laugh,

Hey, you just do the baby way!
Duh-duh, duh-duh—little baby.

Well, I bet you couldn't do it
if you'd had polio! Lonnie slams
the words back at them.
His breath staggers in the telling,
throat constricts, eyes expand, hands clench.
He relives the passion.

He grew up to be a policeman—
father of three sons
and six daughters.
He has championed all of them
just like he did his friend
in first grade.
– Helen

Dad's Plum Tree

We were on the subject
of Dad's green thumb again.

I think if he just stuck an old stick in the ground
it would grow. That's what I said.
It did. He did that. Alan's laugh

69

poured out like a harvest of plums.
Come and look. I followed,
feeling a child again,
striding to match the measure
of my big brother.
Out the kitchen door we went,
through Mom's flower garden,
pausing close to the forgotten fenceline
that connected his yard to theirs.
Dad picked up a stick lying there
on the ground, an old dry stick,
turned it over in his hand,
like he was weighing it,
his hand pumping up and down,
measuring it with his eyes.
He raised it like a javelin,
thrusting it into the yielding ground
tamped the earth around it with his foot,
then left it, went on to whatever else
he was doing, whatever he had been about.

Ten years gone. Now, in front of us,
blessing that corner of the garden--
a young plum tree,
grown to fifteen feet or so--
exultant blossoms on rich plum wood.
Can we, dry twigs, with such a planting
root and yield?
– Helen

Aunt Doree Went First

Hell, Bill. Whut took yuh so long?

Aunt Doree would say that.
She's one of the ones

70

that's already gone over.
Ma died five years ago and some.
We didn't think Pa would
last a week after she went.

He just keeps sayin'
I'm about ready tuh kick the bucket.
But he's still here, 93 years old,
whittlin' on his canes,
wishin' he was with
his little sweetheart,
'n tellin' a blame for each ache and pain.
But Doree's another story.
She put off gittin' baptized—

didn't want to hurt her ma, who was Catholic.
Guess she thought she'd wait
until her ma died.

But Doree went first.
– Helen

Smell the Greasepaint

He was six when I took him
to the audition for Brecht's
The Good Woman of Setzuan.
You'd think he'd been *born in a trunk*:
his performance was a sensation!

Three years later, I took him to a play.
Afterwards we headed for the green room
to greet my friends. He swayed,
stopped at the top of the stairs,
flung his arms wide,
Ahhh! Just smell the greasepaint.

He helped me run lines for *Ondine*.
After recording it on Alan's tape machine,
we played it back.
Ten year-old Lon was in shock
when his voice sounded like a child.
He had expected to sound
like Wayne or Dad.

Directors seek him out,
keep him busy acting and singing
in their plays. Look closely about him.
There are traces of greasepaint still clinging.
– Helen

Consider The Choice

Eventually all conversations
get into the age thing.
I try to look indignant
when it is my turn to share,
say something like,
Mary Tyler Moore and I . . .

My brother Alan waltzed through
the kitchen on his way out,
stopped to kiss his wife good-bye,
then flew out the door,
an eagle, eager to soar.

Waving, he started the car,
pulled onto the street,
collided with a pick-up truck.

It took less than a minute from good-bye
to goodbye. He was fifty-nine.
– Karen

Irises and Peonies for Decoration Day

For Alan

The ritual of decorating graves
repeats yearly, like rows of headstones.
Irises oozed purple ink,
drip, dripping.
Full blossoms shrank
and curled into clenched fists;
infant blossoms unfurled flags
from the same pods.

Alan was the oldest.
His shadow encompassed mine.
From Dad's garden we garnered
first flowers, apt offering
for the end of May, his birthday.
Behind rows of irises
peonies bowed copious heads.
Snowball bushes lined the fence.
He carried full buckets of water
to the car sloshing, washing my feet.
We immersed the wounded stems.

Years later, a July morning sun
exploded in glaring brilliance
over the mountains. Blinded,
his car rocketed out of orbit,
intersected with another.
Petals of time scattered
like confetti from Roman candles.
That was twenty years ago.

I continue to bring irises
that stain the headstone and grass
with their mute mourning.

– Helen

Tell Mama To Wait

Before the August sun blooms,
lighting my day,
I get the Sisters' summons.

You had better come.

Four other times I answered the call,
four times a resurrection.
Half in jest, I say,

Tell her to wait until I get there.

Preparing, I wade in heavy desert sands,
nine hours of hurried waiting.
The plane drones on
while faster-than-light-speed yesterdays
jet by, flashing images on my mind screen;
bursts of dormant memories retrieved
like mothballed winter woolens.

She waits for me.
I see her submerged in prelude sleep,
fading like an Arizona sunset.
She's smaller than I remember,
delicate as her porcelain doll,
both worn from loving.
Reality pierces my heart.

From the hollow place where journeys
such as this originate, she knows I'm here.
My hands cradle hers, while whispered words
of caring wind their way to her waking.

She gives me twenty minutes.
I'm at Mama's house, and it is dark.
— *Karen*

The Viewing In The Parlor

April blows through open parlor windows,
freshens air dank as Uncle Jesse's cellar.
The sofa, straight-back chairs,
and china cupboard filled with tired dishes
bunch together to clear the floor
for the dance, to make room for her.

Shrouded in *ifs* her husband
braces himself against the coffin,
his hand stroking the mound-shaped lid,
finds comfort in its polished surface.
Like weaned puppies yearning milk,
four children huddle close around him.

My ten-year-old wisdom denied,
I go with Aunt Bess to the viewing.
The bereaved, the curious, and others come,
bearing nourishment for empty stomachs,
vacant hearts.

In library voices, they console him,
pat little heads, smooth neglected hair.
They two-step the dirge by her forever bed:
stop mid-step, click a tongue, wipe a tear.

She leaves me, joins the slow-motion line
of mourners, dabs her eyes
with a brassy yellow handkerchief.
Curious, I stand alone, watch the body
like a robin watches stillborn eggs,
wait for movement, for sound, for life.

Years, stacked like old books
piled four decades high,
find me standing at the corner

of my mother's casket, watching.
I cry for me, weep for children everywhere
whose loss is mine, cry at last
for the children in the parlor who watched,
and waited.
– Karen

About Faces

It's the getting ready for the day, every day,
that's the hardest.
I started *putting on my face* at fifteen,
that's sixteen-thousand-four-hundred-
twenty-five attempts, minus fifty or so.
I struggle to fix my hair the way it wants.

Decades older, doing the face requires
a four-times magnifying mirror,
a myriad of magician's potions:
creams to slow the aging, makeup
to cover years. And magic wands:
pencils, liners, mascara, colors for shading.
Colors that cannot shade the guilt
of abundance so different
from the sparse store of helps Mama used.

At fifty, mother became an Avon Lady.
In my mirror, I see her shadow styling
long hair in its usual twist; using her only wand,
a brown Mabelline pencil to shape brows.
But now, from her sample case, lipstick.
And for the first time, perfume, a drop
on a pinch of cotton dabbed behind each ear,
then buried deep in disavowed cleavage.

At eighty, Mama is frayed around the edges,
worn smooth as a child's favorite toy.

Years earlier, she stopped doing her face
except for cold cream twice-a-day, which keeps
her ageless and beautiful like when we were
saplings growing close together in fertile ground. Her hair
is bobbed the way it was when Daddy cut it.

It's the getting ready for the day, today,
that's the hardest. I go through the routine
without magic, mirror dark as an August storm.
My sisters apply color on our Mother's lips,
now lullaby silent; comb her hair,
use the Mabelline pencil on her brows.

And for the last time, a trace of Cotillion.
– *Karen*

Don't Ever Pierce Your Ears

Mama said that a thousand times,
maybe more. I asked her once if. . .
Absolutely not!
She would never allow
me to be seen with holes in my ears,
people would label me a tramp.
Worse, a carnival worker.

After that, every time I saw
someone with pierced ears,
gasps escaped my pursed lips.
In high school, I knew she was right.
Only the girls with peroxided hair
who drank Coke for breakfast
had pierced ears.

Eventually, friends succumbed
to fashion, but not me.

Helen defied the rule; four daughters,
and she was the bravest.

Mama's wisdom, willed
to my three daughters,
fell on deaf ears.
Using wily ways, they convinced
their father to take them to the mall
while I worked, then sashayed
into my office flaunting silver studs
decorating virgin earlobes.

I was fifty when Mama died.
On display, a sly smile on her lips,
friends and family filed by the matriarch.
Below her coifed hair, gold earrings
dangled from pierced ears.

– *Karen*

Plowman

Luke 9:62 ... *No man, having put his hand to the plough, and*
looking back, is fit for the kingdom of God.

With hands hard on the harrow
his eyes would shoot ahead,
fix on a mark the far side of the field.
He pushed forward, his weight leaning
as though heading into wind;
measured steps, marched a drumbeat cadence.
Rows advanced, arrow straight.

After a stroke we borrowed a walker
to steady him. He didn't get
the idea it was to support him,
instead he pushed it ahead,
bearing down with his hands on the plow.

Do you see how straight those rows are?
He used to question each one,
but children couldn't comprehend
what it means to fix your eye on the lodestar,
move forward unwaveringly.
No trembling to the right,
no fumbling to the left,
just straight ahead--
once he sets his hand
until he reaches the far side.
Only then, the glance back.
– Helen

Musical Chairs

For me, there was nothing musical
about it. Children followed children
around a line of mismatched chairs
while someone sang, then stopped!

Pleated accordion style, we folded
into each other, scrambled for a place,
one seat eliminated. I tiptoed by,
then lunged at each chair as I paraded,
terrified at the idea of being left out.

Dad sits on the fringe, his chair missing
from the circle, recounts over and again
old yarns about his boyhood: dramas, traumas,
double cousins, chopping wood for winter fires.

We answer him, not looking,

You sure did, Dad—

continue on with our charade.

From the game we laugh through conversation,
songs, and joke-telling at a speed
he can't process.

At intervals, his booming baritone
sings a recollection from sixth grade,
Utah, Star of the West, a song that loops
like broken film at the movies.

The gold band Daddy gave Mama
when they were eighteen, binds ten.
Almost worn through in places,
it graces a chain around my neck.

I know belonging now,
join the song, become part
of the round, bound within the spiral.
We become the circle.
– Karen

Home With A Fancy Name

At first breath we stockpile seconds,
inhale hours, save years and decades,
then when ripe, we lose time,
live with no memory.

Daddy struggles to find his bearings,
stays room-bound,
TV and visitors—his new life.
During family visits, we sing away

the present. Waves lap the reservoirs
of his ninety-three year-old mind,
releasing songs glued someplace inside him
like school drawings hung on classroom walls.

Between meals, in the all-purpose room,
worn-out bodies wear look-alike masks
occupy couches as long as stretch limos—
seas of faces staring desperate space.

They connect momentarily
when someone enters,
someone else's son or daughter
come to call.

How long until he becomes
one of them, lumped on the sofa
waiting for hope
beyond the double doors?

This vacant community,
with no reason to remember,
waits.
– Karen

I Haven't Called You Lately

I often wonder where you are,
whether or when I'm included
in your assignments.
Go see what you can do for Helen.
She's having a hard time this week.

You must be good at angel-ing,
your frail body laid aside,
able to move as fast as thought, now,
tuned in to all eight children,
spouses; forty-nine grandchildren;
great grandchildren,
your increasing posterity.

81

And you don't get tired.

Sometimes I try to be still enough
to hear you whispering,
but mostly I'm rushing
from care to care
hampered by time and gravity.

When I beam my messages
to you, do they bounce off stars?
Pierce through clouds?
Bump into other messages
dispatched through the stratosphere?

I trust there is no interference
of space or time.
This is our shred of eternity.
Cords that bind us together
have no end, no beginning.
Every time is now.
Every where is here.
– Helen

Feeding the Multitude

Air stirs with hints of approaching frost.
A few tenacious leaves cling
where plump plums hung purple
against blue September just a week ago.

I am ready for that perfect moment
when the first snap of turgid apple bursts
in my mouth. I wipe my chin and wonder,
will I ever get my fill of red and gold delicious?

As I scan the orchard, assess my abundance,
I hear again my father's words,

It's a sin to let such good fruit go to waste.

I remember how tirelessly he picked,
how generously he shared,
try to follow his pattern:
eat all I can, reach all I can,
stock my cellar, beg anyone who will,
 to come and pick. Still
great beauties already rot underfoot,
tree tops hang heavy with unreachable plenty.

Doing dishes at the sink, my window view
takes in the orchard. First sprinkles
of powdered sugar snow dust the ground,
lighten branches where too many blessings,
beginning to wrinkle, still dangle.

Suddenly a shadow across the sun
draws my eyes to the sky. A multitude
of starlings wave like a great scarf
shaping itself to the wind.
The cloud ebbs and flows
and finally umbrellas my property,
descends and covers my trees
like iron filings on magnets.

After pecking and gorging,
at some invisible command, the birds rise
in concert and are again airborne.

I laugh out loud, give wings to my guilt,
and send it to fly with the flock.
– Mary

Willie's Willow Song

To every thing there is a season . . . Eccl. 3: 1

Wearing an intricate weave of gold
over jaded green,
willows abide as the last bastion
of hope for prolonging fall.

Seasoned branches bend low,
benevolently brush the ground,
struggle against inevitable November.
After a short sleep,
they will be first to salute the spring.

Dad was a willow,
kin to trees he planted across
the fertile valley. He stretched
his autumn, accumulated todays,
gathered his children in zealous arms.

Nearly a century of circles marked
his time when winter came.
His generous heart yearned for home,
but he wondered the how of no tomorrow.

Shivering in cold air, lingering leaves
fell from his tree, the passing easier
than he could have imagined.

When Daddy bowed to touch
the earth goodbye, we heard the willows
whisper through the moving air,
Well done.

– Karen

About the Authors

Three sisters born during the Depression share rich memories of their family and neighborhood through their growing-up years in Utah County. Helen recalls "Early memories see us gathered around the kitchen table with Dad challenging us on the meaning and spelling of words and Mother sharing the good books she was reading. This was the beginning of our love of words." They credit their focus on poetry to their oldest sister Beverly, who married Max Golightly—actor, teacher, director, and poet. Through him they became involved in poetry and joined the Utah State Poetry Society in the mid-nineties through his encouragement and tutelage. He served as their mentor until his death in April 1997.

Their warm and welcoming personalities encourage others as they share their personal stories. They have won awards for their writing on both the state and national levels and have been published in Nine One One: Poems for September 11, Utah Sings, ByLine Magazine, Poetry Panorama and Encore. All are also engaged in Church service and joyously involved in families and grandmothering.

Mary is a natural storyteller. She has one novel finished and is working on a second, has been writing a variety of children's stories as well as poetry. She excels in flower arranging and gardening. People also flourish under her care and she always has someone living at her home. She welcomes many for soup and sing-alongs. She is proud mother of eight, grandmother of forty-two with a burgeoning of great grandchildren.

Karen's book Bread and Milk and Music, from which we took our title, took third place in the 2005 Utah State Poetry Society Manuscript competition. Though her family and children are her priority, she is glad to have time at this phase of her life to write poetry "to nourish her soul." She is continually nourishing and nurturing others with her hospitality, and poetry. She was a successful business executive, having owned several franchises. She also worked as spokesperson and vice president of training for a nationally known diet program.

Helen earned degrees in dance, English and ESL. She is serving a second term as president of the Word Weavers, Utah Valley Chapter of the USPS. She has placed second and third in the USPS manuscript competition in 1999 and 2007, and was a finalist in the 2003 Byline Magazine Poetry Chapbook Competition. She is currently editor of the USPS newsletter Poet Tree.

Please forgive our failures and accept our poems as an offering to all who find themselves in our poetry.

Additional copies of this book
are available.

Please direct requests or inquiries to

Karen Gibson
2124 North 220 East
Provo, Ut 84604